Seasons of the Bighorn

Great American Rivers

Seasons of the Bighorn

By George Kelly

Photographs by Barry & Cathy Beck

WILLOW CREEK PRESS

MINOCQUA, WISCONSIN

All photographs © by Barry and Cathy Beck, except: pp. 29,
51, 58, 64, 79, 86 © by George Kelly.

Edited by Kim Leighton
Designed by Patricia Bickner Linder

Published by Willow Creek Press
PO Box 147, Minocqua, WI 54548

For information on other Willow Creek titles,
write or call 1-800-850-WILD

Library of Congress Cataloging-in-Publication Data:

Kelly, George
        Seasons of the Bighorn / by George Kelly ;
photographs by Barry & Cathy Beck.
        p.   cm. -- (Great American rivers ; 1)
        ISBN 1-57223-124-6 (hc : alk. paper)
        1. Trout fishing--Bighorn River (Wyo. and Mont.) 2.
Fly fishing--Bighorn River (Wyo. and Mont.) 3. Seasons-
-Bighorn River (Wyo. and Mont.) 4. Trout fishing--
Bighorn River (Wyo. and Mont.)--Pictorial works. 5. Fly
fishing--Bighorn River (Wyo. and Mont.)--Pictorial works.
6. Seasons--Bighorn River (Wyo. and Mont.--Pictorial
works. I. Title. II. Series
SH688.U6K45   1997
799.1'757'0978638--dc21   97-33984
                                               CIP

Printed in Canada.

**Author George Kelly (left) and
photographers Barry and Cathy Beck.**

CONTENTS

ACKNOWLEDGMENTS

Several people were most helpful to me in the production of this book and I offer them my heartfelt thanks. They include Paul Gordon, formerly chief naturalist at Bighorn Canyon National Recreation Area; Ken Fraser and Mike Vaughn, biologists with the Montana Department of Fish, Wildlife and Parks; Tim Felchle supervisor of Reservoir and River Operations for the Bureau of Reclamation's Montana area office; Dan Gustafson, research scientist at Montana State University; and Jo Newhall, my wife, without whom this book would never have been written.

INTRODUCTION

SOME YEARS AGO I WROTE that the Bighorn stands as a nonpareil among North American trout streams. Nothing that has happened in the years since has caused me to change my mind. Indeed I am more convinced than ever that this is the case, and my conviction grows with the passing of the seasons. Shortly after the Bighorn reopened to the angling public in August 1981, noted Montana angler George Anderson asked rhetorically, as the title of an article in *Fly Fisherman* magazine, "The Bighorn: Is it the Best?" He wrote that while only time and experience could provide a definitive answer to this question, preliminary evidence suggests that it well might be.

The minority trout on the Bighorn, the rainbow is nonetheless available in healthy numbers and sizes.

Fifteen years have passed and time has indeed given us some perspective and produced some answers to this question. I think it is now fair to say that not only is the Bighorn a nonpareil among North American trout streams but that it is, by any measure, among the best in the world. The evidence for this assertion is persuasive.

If one accepts the thesis that a great part of the reason that we fish for trout is to catch them, then one of the measures of a great stream should be that it is home to a significant number of trout. That is to say that we can fish with confidence, secure in the knowledge that we are not wasting our time on unproductive waters, and that our success or lack thereof will depend mainly on our angling skills.

According to Montana Department of Fish, Wildlife and Parks biologists, in the first 13 river miles below Yellowtail Dam the Bighorn is home to over 5,000 catchable trout per mile — a very conservative estimate, in my opinion. Still, while the number varies somewhat from year to year depending on stream flow, it is a staggering figure. It indicates that with a few exceptions there are nearly twice as many catchable trout per mile in the Bighorn than in any other trout stream in Montana. If the sheer number of trout available to be caught was the sole criterion for judging the value of a trout stream, then surely the Bighorn would stand tall among its peers.

Fortunately, such is not the case and we must consider the size of its fish as a factor at least as important as mere numbers when judging the relative merits of various trout streams. Who among us would not trade quality for quantity on nine days out of ten? It is well documented that the Bighorn is blessed with an abundance of large trout, and some of them are real monsters. I can recall any number of encounters, usually brief and always memorable, with trout whose size I am reluctant to speculate about here, because their proportions are beyond belief. Suffice it to say that there are some biggies about, and one such was a brown caught by one of our guests a few years ago. He was a wondrous creature, thick and heavy in his maturity and he weighed around ten pounds, according to the scale at the

local grocery store. He has since grown in memory to about 11½ pounds, which is admirable growth for a dead fish, but somewhat less than he would have enjoyed had he remained in the river. This is not to

True leviathans like this monster brown don't come along every day, but there are a good number of them in the Bighorn.

The Bighorn's predictable, stable and relatively few insect species make fly selection easier than you might expect.

say that these leviathans are to be expected on the Bighorn as a daily possibility. They are certainly not. Rather, they should be savored when they do occur as the rarities that they are, and released unharmed with a salute and a prayer that you will meet again. For if the Bighorn has a weakness, it is a lack of large forage species such as the sculpin and some of the larger stonefly nymphs such as *pteronarcys* and *acroneuria,* components of aquatic food chains that regularly produce outsize trout. I've never seen a sculpin or an *acroneuria* on the river and the few *pteronarcys* I've seen could have been transported to the river in an itinerant angler's boat.

There are rivers in Montana such as the Beaverhead and some lakes tucked away throughout the state that

regularly produce these fish of fervid dreams, and if you want to catch a "double digit" trout try one of these places. If you have the skill and put in sufficient time your efforts will likely be rewarded. Better yet, try New Zealand or Tierra del Fuego. You can scarcely miss in "the land of fire." Of course, it helps to have a good bit of discretionary cash laying around.

The Bighorn, on the other hand, is everyman's river. It is easy to get to, and when you get there accommodations range from inexpensive to free to opulent and expensive. The point is that you have a choice and the trout, egalitarian creatures that they are, don't care what choice you make. Though I've noticed over the years that, all things being equal, browns seem to prefer an angler dressed in at least a bit of tweed, and rainbows most assuredly prefer a ball cap that says "Joe's Bait Shop" or something of that nature. This preference doubtless has to do with their respective heritages.

Having decried the lack of truly outsized trout on the Bighorn, I must hasten to add that growth rates for its trout are just short of phenomenal. This spring's six-inch rainbow is next fall's twelve-incher, should he be lucky enough to live so long. Lest you think I've confused multiplication with addition, I lifted these figures from a masters thesis from Montana State University by H. R. Stevenson. Rich, a Livingston-based guide and artist, actually went out in the spring, tagged and measured certain fish and then measured them again in the fall.

These are the results he noted.

Of course these growth rates are not sustainable in terms of inches gained over time, but the reality of the situation is pretty special. The average four-year-old fish approaches

If you're a dedicated flyfisher, you should be in this picture at least once during your angling career.

A year-round trout fishery, the Bighorn is a classic wading angler's stream — except during spring's high flows.

twenty inches and is thick and broad of beam. So much for the quality of the trout in the river. There are lots of them and some of them are large.

We all know trout fishing is not merely a numbers game and we anglers are not or shouldn't be bean counters. This being the case, we must look further for the source of the Bighorn's magic and the spell that it casts over those who know and love it.

Is it the fact that the Bighorn is blessed with moderate weather more or less year-round — a veritable banana belt by Montana standards — making it possible to cast to rising fish a good percentage of the days of the year? Or is it the great insect hatches that assure that the trout will rise sometimes hour after hour and day after day? Is it the fact it is an easy river to wade, a factor I would surely have scoffed at twenty years ago and just as surely cherish today. Or maybe it's just the sheer peace and beauty of the river and its place in the sun. I doubt that any of those factors alone can claim the river such a special place in the hearts of the legion of anglers who yearly heed its call. Rather, it is the combination of these singular and remarkable elements that results in the special magic of the Bighorn. This book is an attempt to share the understanding of that magic.

Bighorn River
–Montana

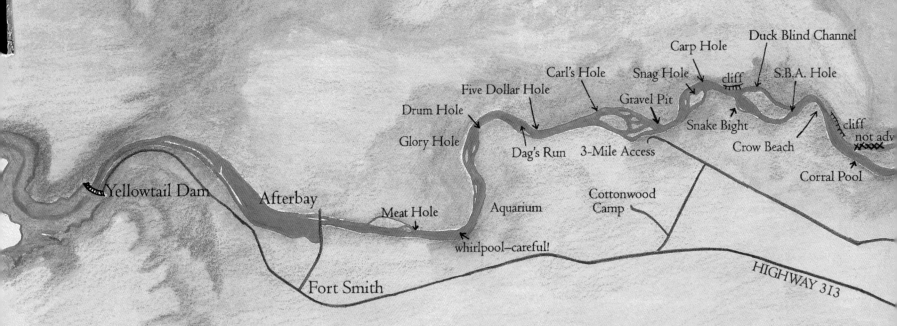

Duck Blind Channel

Carp Hole

Carl's Hole

Snag Hole

cliff

S.B.A. Hole

Five Dollar Hole

Gravel Pit

Drum Hole

Snake Bight

Glory Hole

Dag's Run

3-Mile Access

Crow Beach

cliff
not adv

Corral Pool

Yellowtail Dam

Afterbay

Meat Hole

Aquarium

Cottonwood
Camp

whirlpool–careful!

Fort Smith

HIGHWAY 313

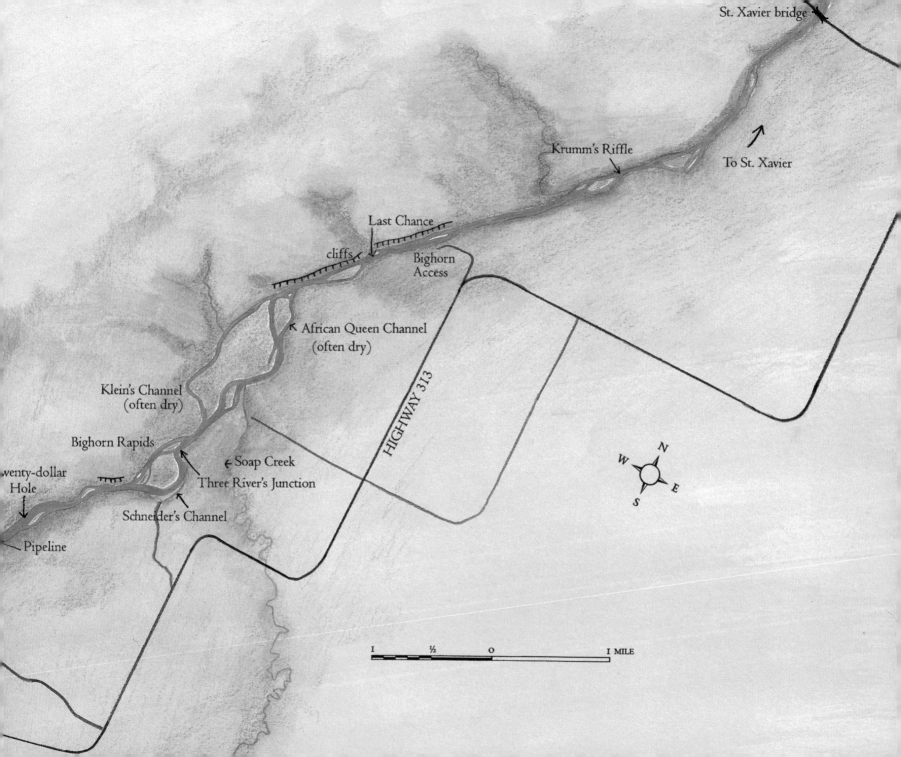

St. Xavier bridge

Krumm's Riffle

To St. Xavier

Last Chance

cliffs

Bighorn
Access

African Queen Channel
(often dry)

Klein's Channel
(often dry)

HIGHWAY 313

Bighorn Rapids

← Soap Creek

Three River's Junction

wenty-dollar
Hole

Schneider's Channel

Pipeline

N
W   E
S

½   O   I MILE

HISTORY

HIGH ON THE EASTERN FLANK of the Wind River Mountains in Wyoming myriad tiny rills and brooks begin their long journey to the Atlantic Ocean. Their individuality is soon lost in larger streams and creeks which in turn converge to form the Wind River. After leaving the mountains the Wind River flows straight north into Boysen Reservoir. Then it spills out of the dam and into the Owl Creek Mountains, where it has cut a gorge that exposes 500 million years of geology. As the river leaves Wind River Canyon and enters the Bighorn Basin just south of Thermopolis, Wyoming, at the so-called "Wedding of the Waters," its name changes to the Bighorn River. There is no

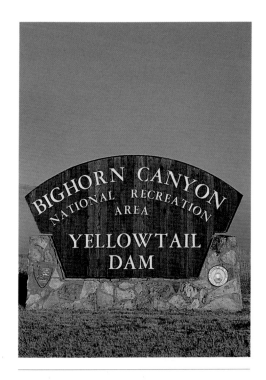

A mediocre trout river in its wild state, the Yellowtail Dam transformed the Bighorn into one of the finest trout streams in the world.

convergence of rivers here, or anything to indicate a reason for the name change and I can find no explanation. I think it may have to do with the name applied by the Indian tribes whose historical territory the river crossed. The "Wedding of the Waters" is approximately at the southern boundary of what was once "Crow Country" and it seems reasonable that the Crows must have had a name for a waterway that more than likely played an important role in their lives. The same can be said for the river to the south that flows through the territory of the Shoshone. It's also possible that the earliest white men, confused by the complex geology of the terrain and unable to understand how a river could flow through a mountain range,

assumed that they were indeed two rivers and named them accordingly.

The Bighorn then continues north through the Bighorn Basin and the northern end of the Bighorn Mountains in Montana to its confluence with the Yellowstone River, seventy miles across the northern plains. It is this area just north of Bighorn Canyon that is the principal focus of this book. It is worth taking a brief look at the geology of the canyon and surrounding area to give us a better understanding of the river that means so much to us as anglers today.

As the river flows across the Bighorn Basin of northern Wyoming it does so in large meanders through non-resistant Cretaceous and Tertiary rock formations which have little effect on the river's chemistry. As it hits the mountains, however, its meanders are incised into deep canyons in resistant, slightly folded Paleozoic limestone. The operative word here is, of course, "limestone," and from one end of Bighorn Canyon to the other, the river is constantly being enriched by the very rock through which it flows, from Gallatin Limestone of Cambrian age up through Bighorn Dolomite and Madison Limestone of the Mississippian System. As an adjunct to your angling adventures, a trip through Bighorn Canyon by boat is not only a trip through altogether lovely scenery, it is also an awe-inspiring trip through time. If you turn off your boat engine in some sheltered little side canyon you can literally hear and see the earth being born as oozing and dripping water forever transfigures rock that seems so permanent.

But such digressions aside, we are concerned with limestone and its effect on the river. As water dissolves, limestone and various carbonates are formed, increasing the alkalinity of the water. This high alkalinity, in the neighborhood of pH 7.4-7.8, sets the stage for boundless numbers of freshwater invertebrates that call the Bighorn home.

High alkalinity alone would not account for the tremendous density of these invertebrates, for environmental factors such as turbidity, formation of anchor ice in winter, and the disruption of the river bottom by extremely high springtime

Looking downstream from the Afterbay Dam. Many anglers prefer the first three miles below the afterbay.

Shortly after the Vernal Equinox, the Bighorn is characterized by blue skies, willing trout and Montana on its best behavior.

flows would have seriously limited their populations.

We must look at the building of a dam, one of the most vilified creations in the history of the American West, depending, of course, on your point of view, in this case Yellowtail Dam, for its role in changing a wild and lovely but relatively unproductive river into what it is today. Not so wild perhaps, but still lovely and surpassingly generous in its bounty for the angler.

Construction of Yellowtail Dam was started by Morrison-Knudsen in 1961 and was completed in 1967. Water storage began on November 4, 1965. Somewhere in the planning stage of the dam serendipity raised its fortunate head, because unlike many dams, this one came complete with an afterbay dam, which has the salubrious effect of mitigating peak-power-demand discharges from Yellowtail, thus insuring stable flows in the river. We'll take a closer look at some of the technical aspects of the dam a bit later, but prior to the dam's construction the Bighorn was basically a prairie river and the fish population consisted mostly of various warm-water species including suckers, goldeye, carp, and chubs. Small populations of brown trout were present near the mouths of some feeder streams. Brown trout have never been planted in the Bighorn, so the huge current population must have come from this small but apparently thriving population in and about various feeder creeks. Lime Kiln creek, a tributary of the

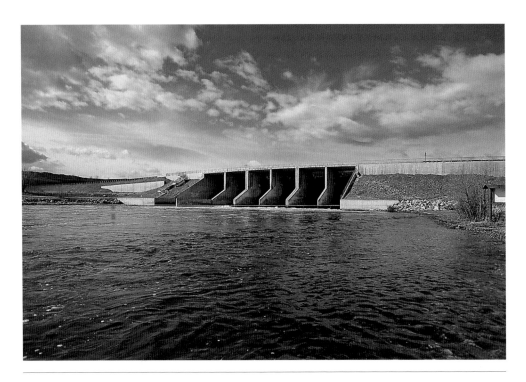

The Afterbay Dam is critical to the Bighorn because it keeps water flows — hence the trouts' food chain — nearly constant.

of 38,000 cfs (cubic feet per second) to a low of 220 cfs. The effect of these remarkable flows on stream life is highly destructive, and it is, from an angler's viewpoint, well that they are history. In addition to ending these huge variations in stream flows the dam also moderated water temperatures in the river, further contributing to its desirability as a home for trout.

Though nearly all of the effects of the dam from a trout fisherman's standpoint have been positive, some have not — one of these is nitrogen bubble disease. This disease is caused by supersaturation of nitrogen in river water as it passes over the Afterbay Dam. Various methods to deal with this phenomenon have been tried and others discussed, but all have been

Yellowtail Dam afterbay, has a good population of brown trout, for example. In keeping with a prairie river, the Bighorn at one time experienced extreme variations in stream flows, from an historic high shelved at least temporarily as being impractical or too expensive. This situation has been largely mitigated in recent years by an agreement between the Bureau of Reclamation and the Montana Department of Fish, Wildlife and Parks. According to the terms of the agreement, the Bureau of Reclamation has agreed to use the radial gates instead of the sluice gates of the Afterbay Dam in regulating river flows, significantly reducing nitrogen supersaturation. Doing so limits power-generating capacity, because relatively high water levels must be maintained in the afterbay in order to use the radial gates. By comparison, the sluice gates can be used at any afterbay water level.

This solution has proved to be remarkably effective and according to biologists Ken Fraser and Mark Vaughn of the Montana Department of Fish, Wildlife and Parks, there is now very little evidence of nitrogen bubble disease more than a couple of hundred yards below the afterbay. Moreover, it is, for all practical purposes, nonexistent at the Three Mile river access. The down side of this agreement is, of course, that it will go out the window should power demands exceed Yellowtail's generating capacity according to the parameters of the agreement. This is as it should be, since no one could reasonably argue that the well being of a few fish should take precedence over the well being of people who depend on the power generated by the dam. Let us hope that in the not too distant future a more permanent solution to this

The Afterbay Dam river access in the background is an easy place to launch a drift boat and a day that fly-fishing dreams are made of.

Although not native to the Bighorn, rainbow trout have thrived and flourished since early stocking programs gave them a foothold.

problem can be found. I should mention here that I view this agreement as a real glimmer of hope for the future of angler-Bureau of Reclamation relations. I doubt that this could have happened a few years ago, and that the voice of the angler, even though ably amplified by the Department of Fish, Wildlife and Parks, would have gone crying in the wilderness of bureaucratic indifference.

As the new reservoir created by the Yellowtail Dam filled, the Montana Department of Fish, Wildlife and Parks began a vigorous stocking program, which resulted in 105,000 cutthroat trout and 500,000 rainbow trout being placed in the river and the afterbay between May 1966 and August 1973. Over the years many more hundreds of thousands of

rainbows were planted, though the planting of cutthroat was discontinued in 1972. Apparently they didn't compete well with browns and rainbows. I have never seen a cutthroat in the river, though I've talked to a few anglers who have, though not since the early 1980s.

Though the stocking program was an unqualified success, concurrent research by personnel of the Montana Department of Fish, Wildlife and Parks, particularly that of Dick Vincent's on the Madison River, was strongly suggesting that stocking wasn't the panacea for all fisheries it was thought to be. That, in fact, stocked fish were detrimental to self-sustaining wild trout populations. The strain of rainbow being planted in the river at the time was

Angler Sam Battaglino releases a nice trout on the 'Horn. Catch-and-release fishing is the linchpin of today's great fishing on this great river.

the so-called Arlee strain from the state hatchery in Arlee, Montana. This was in many ways a great fish, capable of prodigious growth to Bunyanesque size. Those of us who were lucky enough to have fished the river in the first few years after it reopened still recall with unabashed nostalgia those whoppers we caught and, particularly, those that bade us *adios* as they headed around the bend and into memory. The problem with the Arlee rainbow was that it had been bred as a fall spawner, and spawning in the fall does not seem to work for rainbows in the Bighorn. The reasons for this are unclear and the Arlee rainbow remains a vital part of the Department of Fish, Wildlife and Park's stocking programs throughout the state.

It was time to look elsewhere for a rainbow trout that could truly make the Bighorn its home and become, for all practical purposes, a native. This has since transpired and the last rainbow was planted in the Bighorn in 1986. The river now enjoys a spring-spawning, highly successful strain of rainbow which apparently competes successfully with the river's ubiquitous brown trout. According to electro-shocking studies, in fact, its numbers exceed that of brown trout in some areas downstream from the Bighorn fishing access, a dozen miles below Afterbay Dam. This strain seems to be the offspring of fish from Lake de Smet in Wyoming, Willow Creek Reservoir, and the Madison River with perhaps a smattering of the old Arlee strain thrown in. The

Madison River fish were actually wild trout transplanted by Mike Vaughn and Ken Fraser of the Department of Fish, Wildlife and Parks. The fact that they survived and their offspring are thriving is a testament to the insight and professional skills of people such as Dick Vincent, Mike, and Ken. Neither can it hurt that the Bighorn River is a most accommodating place to be if you are a rainbow trout.

Yellowtail Dam named after Robert Yellowtail, a Crow Indian leader and longtime superintendent of the Crow Reservation, sits squarely in the heart of what remains of "Crow Country." As the lake created by the dam filled, it inundated many prehistoric sites of archeological significance. The record, however, has

Wildflowers enliven this view of "Bighorn Country" looking out from the road to OK E Beh.

apparently been preserved by the Smithsonian Institution which had teams studying in the canyon before it was flooded.

Who lived in Bighorn Canyon? When did they live there? And what

The country surrounding the Bighorn River is largely the Crow Indian Reservation, the transition zone between the Rockies and the plains.

winters in the canyon and followed spring as it marched up the west side of the canyon and into the Pryor Mountains. Why they chose to live only on the Pryor Mountain side and not in the Bighorn Mountains is purely a matter of speculation, but I think it must have had to do with the number of buffalo that called the Pryors home.

The area from Dryhead Creek to what is now the town of Pryor is thought to have held the largest concentration of buffalo on the Northern Plains. Dryhead Creek drains a portion of the Pryors and flows into the reservoir about fifteen miles upstream from the dam. One buffalo jump found on the Hoodoo Creek-Dryhead Creek divide had deposits of buffalo remains sixty feet thick.

became of them? There is evidence that man inhabited the canyon as much as 9,000 years ago. Very little is known about the early residents of Bighorn Canyon but the archeological record indicates that they spent their

These buffalo skulls give Dryhead Creek its name and lends the area a certain eerie mystery. Mysterious to me perhaps but most assuredly home to a race of men whose origin and history are known only to the ancient hills and cliffs over which they once chased the buffalo.

Some historians think that these dwellers of mountain and canyon were the progenitors of the Shoshone Indians. But it's likely we'll never know and their place in Bighorn Canyon was eventually occupied by the Crow Indians who rode into the area late in the 18th century. The Crows have been here ever since, though prior to their great chief, Plenty Coup, and his assistance to General Crook at the battle of the Rosebud the Crow had been driven far to the west by the Sioux and only ventured east of the river in strong war parties. History indicates that it was the leverage thus gained by Plenty Coup that enabled him to bargain effectively for the return of land east of the Bighorn to the Crows to become part of what is now the Crow Reservation. It's a sad note that this reservation which once contained over 38 million acres of Montana and Wyoming has been reduced to a little over 2 million acres. Prime land to be sure, rich in natural resources, but only a ghost of what it was when their world was limitless and the Crows were wild and free. The Crows call themselves Absalooke or "Children of the Big Beaked Bird" and at one time they were surely as free as birds following the buffalo through a land that must

A handsome people, the Crow Indians figure prominently in the Bighorn River's past, present and future.

Bighorn country is cattle country. If you come upon a driven herd, it's best to stop your vehicle until a cowboy waves you through.

have been a paradise where the Rockies meet the plains.

It is at this point precisely where the mountains meet the plains and the Bighorn River emerges from its canyon through those mountains that is the site of Yellowtail Dam. The dam is 1.5 million cubic yards of concrete that stands 525 feet high and 1,480 feet across. It has a spillway in the left abutment which has an intake controlled by two 64-foot radial gates and a discharge capacity of 92,000 cfs. Bighorn Lake, behind the dam, has a capacity of 1.37 million acre feet and a conservation capacity of 613,672 acre feet. At an elevation of 3,657 feet, the reservoir has a surface area of 17,300 acres. In actual practice however the lake has surface area which is considerably less because 3,657 feet is 17 feet above what is called "flood pool." The Bureau of Reclamation endeavors to keep the lake below this level.

The stated purposes of the dam are irrigation, flood control, hydroelectric power, and recreation —

though not necessarily in that order except, of course, for recreation. Recreation assumes its place at the bottom of the pile, though there are signs that this may be changing. The Yellowtail Dam emerged out of controversy. And given current political, economic, and environmental considerations it is likely that it would never be built, according to Rob Schroeder, manager of the Reclamation Bureau's Montana Area office. Nonetheless, the dam is a fact, and for those of us who fish in the river it is a blessing.

The construction of the dam and a U.S. Supreme Court decision in 1981 must be considered the two most important factors in the creation of the Bighorn River fishery as we know it today. The case upon which this

decision was based started in a prosaic enough manner in 1975, with the arrest of one James Junior Finch, by tribal authorities for trespassing on tribal land while he was fishing the river. He was found guilty in tribal

Tourism — including trout fishing — is becoming equally important to Montana's economy as mining, cattle ranching and logging.

Every summer the Crow Indians
and many others participate in the
reenactment of the Battle of the
Bighorn. It's a stirring experience
that's not to be missed.

court and decided to appeal. His
conviction was overturned in federal
District Court in Billings by Judge
James Battin. The Crow Tribe
appealed Battin's decision to the 9th
Circuit Court of Appeals in San
Francisco and won a reversal. Earlier,
the state of Montana had joined the
case, and with the Circuit Court's
decision for the Crows, Montana
sued their representative, the U.S.
government, appealing the case to the
U.S. Supreme Court. On March 24,
1981 Justice Potter Stuart delivered the
opinion of the court. The state of
Montana had prevailed. In a 6-3
landmark decision, the justices ruled
that the state of Montana owns the
Bighorn river bed and therefore the
Crow Tribe has no right to regulate
fishing upon its waters.

Though I suppose it is presump-
tuous of me, I have read the decision
carefully and were I judging this case
today, I would probably have dissented,
agreeing with Judge Blackmun, who
wrote simply and eloquently for the
minority: "Because I believe that the
United States intended, and the Crow
Nation understood, that the bed of
the Bighorn was to belong to the Crow
Indians, I dissent from so much of the
Court's opinion as holds otherwise."

Immediately below Yellowtail
Dam lies the unincorporated town of
Fort Smith, a rather eclectic collec-
tion of trailer houses, tackle shops,
motels, a general store, a church and a
restaurant, all more or less dependent
on a thriving sportfishing industry.
The town is situated on approximately the site of Fort Smith, one

of three military posts built to protect the Bozeman Trail. The great Sioux War Chief Red Cloud, however, had other ideas for these forts and through constant warfare against them was soon able to negotiate their closure. Fort C.F. Smith, built in 1866, passed into history in 1868 along with Forts Reno and Phil Kearney. Shortly thereafter, Red Cloud and his warriors burned them to the ground and white men left the area. Fierce battles between the Crow and Sioux raged, however, and by 1876 the Crows had been pushed far to the west. About this time, the Crows allied with the U.S. against the Sioux to recover their lost territory in the Bighorns and surrounding country. In this they were successful and the Bighorns remain the spiritual center

of "Crow Country" today. Forty-some miles to the east of Bighorn Canyon, on a low ridge overlooking the Little Bighorn, Crow scouts guided the U.S. Seventh Cavalry, commanded by General George A.

Any flyfisher will know he's in serious trout country by the number of drift boats in Fort Smith, the Bighorn's gateway community.

Rattlesnakes certainly exist in Montana but their threat is overrated. Give them a wide berth and they'll do the same for you.

Custer, to its own fateful date with destiny.

The country around Fort Smith is alive with fascinating history of the Sioux, Crows, soldiers, and mountain men. The museum atop Yellowtail Dam in Bighorn Canyon National Recreation Area is a good place to start a historical tour. It is here you'll learn that Jim Bridger was the first white man to float the Bighorn with a load of furs destined to be made into hats for the gentry of Eastern cities. Today fishing guides, many of whom are spiritual throwbacks to Jim Bridger and his companions in the fur trade, float their drift boats down the river intent on arranging their clients' own particular rendezvous with the trout.

One of the early guides on the Bighorn was a jolly felon by the name of Griz, a misplaced mountain man whose reputation as a teller of tall tales would have made old Jim himself envious. I don't think Griz ever caught a trout under five pounds or shot a duck at under fifty yards. His checks were written on a particularly high quality of rubber and he was last heard of heading for the border with the law in hot pursuit. I know nothing of the Griz before he showed up on the Bighorn, but many of the guides who worked the river in its early days immigrated from various trouty venues around the West, such as the saloons of Livingston, West Yellowstone, Aspen, and Jackson Hole. Most of them came as refugees from a hardscrabble world of short guide seasons and long, cold winters, where they eked out an existence working construction in 20° below, or huddled over a fly-tying desk for days on end. Tying flies for fun is just that. Doing it for a living is most certainly drudgery of the most tedious kind, and to my way of thinking, to be avoided at all costs. Some of these early guides skied professionally in the winter and returned to the Bighorn when the corn turned to slush and trout were once again dimpling in the eddies and runs. Some still do and some are gone for good. Mike Craig has sold his place and become a world traveler, though he still has a house on the river. A.J. is still ski patrolling in the winter and guiding elsewhere. He tells me he's found some places where there are practically no people. If I can get away this summer, I think I'll ask him to show me. Ron Granamen spends

A few fly shops, a restaurant and drift boats are the icons of Fort Smith.

more and more time fishing under the Southern Cross, but maintains his status as one of the best and most sought-after guides on the Bighorn.

This is no minor accolade, since I believe the guides on the Bighorn are

Longtime Bighorn guide Dennis Fisher stands by as Sam Battaglino battles a big one.

standouts in the business. Perhaps this is mere chauvinism, a crass and none-too-subtle blowing of my own horn as a member of that cadre of guides, but I think I can make a good case. To guide on the Bighorn effectively one must be an angling generalist well versed in spring creek tactics as well as able to cope with the mysteries of a large and often opaque river. It won't do, for example, to just chuck a Woolly Bugger at the river bank and hope for the best. One must look deeper and more perceptively into what it is that makes a river tick in order to learn its secrets, and most of its guides, in addition to sharing the attributes of good guides everywhere, are experts in the unique and subtle nuances of the Bighorn. Therefore, it seems silly for a visiting angler to hire a guide who is not headquartered on the Bighorn. Fly fishing has very few absolutes, but one of them is that there is no substitute for local knowledge.

Just as the river has attracted a particularly high quality of guide, so has it attracted a whole galaxy of fly-fishing luminaries, some of whom return to the river year after year. The fact that many of them do so on their own time and at their own expense speaks eloquently for the quality of the river, for some of these individuals have access to the rivers of the world.

No reference to Fort Smith and environs would be complete without mention of Polly's Place, a local restaurant and landmark that arrived on the scene shortly after the Fort Smith anticline. Polly unfailingly serves good food from dawn till dusk. If you fish in the summertime until the caddis hatch is history, you can still get a good meal at Polly's. If the service is a little slow, remember that each meal is prepared to order and that many hungry fishermen descend on Polly's at the same time. Knowledgeable anglers sneak into Polly's in midafternoon when the fishing tends to slow to enjoy an incomparable piece of homemade pie with ice cream and take in a little local color.

Local color abounds in Fort Smith, as it sits in raffish insouciance beneath the brooding Bighorns, host to a kaleidoscope population of cowboys and Indians, fishermen and farmers, most as transient as the Bighorns are permanent.

Known to thousands of Bighorn anglers, Polly's Place is where to get your fill of good food and trout talk.

SPRING

IT'S FEBRUARY AS I WRITE THIS and spring is just around the corner. There's not a red-winged blackbird to be seen and a robin's song is a distant dream. But I did hear a pair of great horned owls calling to each other last night and it's likely they have a nest on an island on the river behind the house. I took a look at the river yesterday, as I often do in the winter, just to check it out and found a few fish rising sporadically to a small hatch of midges — harbingers, I trust, of huge hatches a month from now. I fished the river a couple of days ago on a bright and chilly afternoon and didn't see a rise. I did manage to catch a few by fishing deep along a seam where I could see

Spring weather on the Bighorn can be idyllic or challenging for flyfishers. The trout remain cooperative and don't seem to care either way.

them poised in the current, hunkered close to the bottom the only indication of life or interest a nearly imperceptible opening of their mouths and flaring of their gills as they took some passing tidbit. They wouldn't move an inch in the icy water and the fly had to be right in their face to provoke even a flicker of interest. Slow going, but it was good to be out and I fished as long as the light allowed me to see them in their frigid lies. The single rainbow I caught was a fat and fine performer despite the cold but the browns looked scrawny and haggard after a recent and rigorous spawning season. Rising water temperatures in the months to come will change all this and these same torpid trout will soon be perched on expectant fins, high in the water, eagerly chasing any of a multitude of creatures that happen along.

But for now it is too early. The water's too cold and the sun too low in the sky, for it is still winter. And even though each season has its own clearly defined essence, the passing of one to the other can no more be pinpointed than the river be stopped in its flow. Rivers flow into rivers and rivers into oceans and through the hydrologic cycle back to rivers again. It's the same with the seasons. Winter gives way to spring secure in the knowledge that as the earth turns its turn will come again.

Since it's so difficult to precisely discern the passing of winter into spring from indications in the natural world, maybe we can look at human events to tell us that spring is here

A variety of nymphs will take the Bighorn's trout in the springtime. Each day is usually punctuated by a hatch of midges or blue-winged olives, too.

indeed and that whether or not the groundhog saw his shadow is irrelevant.

As February turns into March new rigs show up in the parking lots of various river accesses and sometimes I find a strange drift boat parked hard by where yesterday I did so well. I've had the river pretty much to myself since last December, and the appearance of an interloper at one of my favorite spots is sure to be viewed with dark suspicion. How did he know those fish were there? I've never seen him before. Must be one of those guides from West Yellowstone or Bozeman or Jackson Hole or Timbuktu, for that matter, scouting out the place so he can bring in a big load of clients in a month or two. Paranoia reigns after a long winter.

Such thinking on the part of local outfitters and guides helps to define the start of spring, and by St. Patrick's Day, human activity on the river is increasing as the days grow warmer. As the Vernal Equinox approaches many an angler will pick a day to initiate his own rite of spring.

If the day is not too bright, and, better yet, if it's snowing lightly, one of the first things this angler will notice if he looks closely at the water's surface will be midges, millions of them. Midges (*Chironomids*) are one of only six or so insects that account for 87 percent of invertebrate life in the river, so their presence is of more than passing interest to anglers. If it's early in the day it's likely that the trout will be ignoring what's on top because most of the activity will be taking place subsurface, and a midge pupa imitation drifted in the seams and slower currents should provide good results. As the day warms slightly our angling friend should begin to notice fish rising here and there to drifting adult midges and clusters of them as they skitter hither and yon across the surface. A properly presented Griffith's Gnat or Midge Cluster ought to produce results, but if it doesn't, it wouldn't hurt to swing a small, dark soft-hackle pattern in front of any trout that shows his snout above the surface. One should watch these fish carefully to ascertain whether or not their noses and mouths are actually breaking the surface. Often they're not, and if this is the case try drifting a pupa

It's a rare day when there's not a midge hatch on the Bighorn.

imitation just under the surface with a small parachute Adams up the tippet eighteen inches or so to act as a strike indicator. It often happens that the fish will take one or the other, and once in a while both at the same

Like all trout rivers, the Bighorn fishes best when you know what they're taking. Here, Barry Beck seines for clues.

abundance of life. I don't think it's pushing a point to suggest that the numbers are stellar in their magnitude and have to be witnessed over a period of time to be appreciated.

Another insect that begins to show up after the sun has risen a bit in its arc across the sky is the ubiquitous blue-winged olive, known far and wide across the West as a "super hatch." Our blue-winged olive is *Baetis tricaudatis,* according to Jim Brammer who did his masters thesis on the subject. *Baetis* is another one of those taxa whose numbers make up such a huge part of the biomass in the river. However, I don't think its importance comes close to approaching that of the *Chironomids.* The Bighorn's *Baetis* seem to be cyclical and its numbers ebb and flow

time, which is always good for a few laughs. This midge activity on the Bighorn, while it reaches its peak in spring and late fall, goes on day after day until one can only marvel at how the river can sustain such a super-in response to some mysterious riverine rhythms I can't even pretend to understand. Suffice it to say that some years the Bighorn has many and some years it doesn't. Those years of plenty have provided many memorable days.

One thing can be said of the blue-winged olive is that it is an insect of crummy weather. But not too crummy; if the wind is blowing you won't do well with a dry fly, though you may do fine with a nymph. Size 18 Pheasant Tails, RS2s, and anything else you choose to tie that looks about like the natural will do nicely. A dry CDC *Baetis* pattern with the wing cut down and fished subsurface is deadly.

The kind of day that really brings the trout up to blue-winged olives is one of those common hallmarks of springtime in the Rockies and adjacent plains — cold and drizzly with some nice juicy snowflakes falling from a leaden sky. Days like this are the stuff of dreams, as every fish in the river tries to eat as if he'll never again get the chance. One wants to be close by when it's springtime and the olives are on the water.

One of the intriguing aspects of prairie rivers as they traverse an otherwise sere landscape is that they act as lush arteries for a host of migrating birds. As a consequence, the Bighorn becomes a birder's dream in the spring, a sort of ornithological Eldorado, as feathered creatures of many species use it as pipeline to the north. This pipeline starts filling early with the return of many species

The Bighorn River corridor is a haven for migrating birds and resident birds alike. Swallows are seasonal visitors.

A flock of ducks looks for a place to spend the night as the sun sets on the 'Horn.

of ducks and it stays more or less full until the last shorebird heads for the tundra in late May or early June. Of course the river bank is home to many species that nest and raise their young in its riparian margins, Many eastern birds find the western limit of their range among the Bighorn's stream-side willows and cottonwoods. Take a few moments while you're on the river to tune into the sounds of spring and the beginning of nature's year. This avian chorus reaches its peak in late May and early June and as you float along you'll hear wrens and warblers, meadow-larks, thrushes, and chats. Canada geese scold from the islands as they shepherd their newly hatched balls of yellow fuzz away from your approaching boat and out of harm's way.

A legion of cock pheasants, resplendent in breeding plumage, crow and cackle and generally raise a fuss as they announce their lust to hens skulking nearby. If nature is benevolent and a late spring snow doesn't force them off their nests, the hens will produce a robust crop of young, which in turn will produce grins on the faces of next fall's wing-shooters. Pheasants are everywhere along the Bighorn and so are killdeer, striking in their plumage of brown, muted orange, black, and white. They're here to nest on the river's many gravel bars, but sometimes their plans meet with unexpected and violent interruptions.

One day I was standing on a rocky bar fishing an adjacent run, when I heard the unmistakable sound of air rushing through wings — something like a small jet plane cruising by at a range of maybe two feet. The bird had undoubtedly taken a pass at me and by the time I looked up it was 100 feet away and climbing steeply. It continued its climb to an apogee of several hundred feet from which point it dove in an elliptical arc culminating at an unfortunate killdeer that happened to be sharing the gravel bar with me. Without missing a wing beat, the peregrine stuck out a foot, snatched the killdeer off the bar, and rolled up into a cottonwood across the river and proceeded to dine at his leisure, oblivious to my presence. This vignette, though it took only fifteen seconds, was a matter of life and death, at once brutal and magnificent, and I was privileged to be a witness. Such scenes, though rarely observed, occur daily along the river as part of its eternal ebb and flow.

Somewhere in that ebb and flow of specific speed, and in gravel of specific size, the rainbows are spawning. They begin in late March or early April, when water temperatures are still inordinately cold, and continue through May and into June. Browns spawn all over the river and their redds are everywhere.

Fishing close to the banks is productive on the Bighorn. Such spots offer aquatic and terrestrial insects and a reduced water flow.

In many parts of the country this rainbow trout would be a trophy. On the Bighorn trout this size are referred to as "nice."

it's perfectly legal to fish for these spawners, it seems to me that sportsmanship and regard for a great fish would dictate that we exercise restraint. It can't be good for a fish already stressed from the rigors of spawning to be dragged off its redd and released some yards downstream. Nor can it be good for the redds themselves to be disturbed by size 12 wading brogues attached to some mindless and greedy dolt with a fly rod in hand. Let us hope that in the future fewer and fewer anglers feel compelled to satisfy their piscatorial greed by fishing for a magnificent fish who at the time of spawning is only a shadow of its usual self and needs all the consideration and protection it can get. So much for my soapbox. Springtime and the river is not the

Rainbows seem to have more specific requirements, and their redds are in the same places year after year. Local anglers and guides know this and avoid such places for the most part, but some anglers do not. Although time for such a diatribe. Better to go with the flow, finding solace in the fact that the world is once again new and its possibilities are limitless, if only for a time. The same can be said of the river. Last fall's algae and drifting weeds are only a memory and the river flows in crystalline grace between banks lined with the pastel promise of a new season. Pale pinks, yellows, and dainty whites mingle with an ephemeral and electric green and speak of future wild plums, currants, and chokecherries.

If conditions are just right, that is if sufficient moisture combines with just the right amount of sunshine and warmth, the river islands provide an abundance of that elusive object of epicurean dreams, the morel mushroom. Some years they're here

and some years they're not, and if you should notice anglers and guides shuffling about the islands like myopic drunks you'll know the objects of their quest. A few years ago practically no one was aware of this largess of the gods of spring and the practice of morel hunting was limited to a few sneaky and tight-lipped guides who were also semi-legendary with a frying pan. Apparently they weren't sneaky enough, however, and last year (a great year for morels) the islands were swarming with neoprene-clad anglers who had swapped their fly rods for collecting bags. Better be out early if you want your morels.

Just as winter eases into spring with no discernible break so does spring flow into summer. But I think the seasonal transition is less subtle as

In good years the Bighorn's islands conceal an abundance of the greatly prized wild morel mushroom.

far as the river is concerned. Almost over night it seems the blue-winged olives and midges are history and no insect providing dry-fly fishing immediately replaces them. Water temperatures are still fairly cold and it's almost as if the river takes a breather in anticipation of the hot and frantic activity of summer.

It's an altogether lovely time to be on the river, this ephemeral hiatus between spring and summer, with few fish rising and fewer fishermen fishing for them. This is fortunate or unfortunate, depending upon your point of view. If you're a dry-fly purist this is not the time to be on the Bighorn. But if you like to fish in relative solitude and don't mind drifting a nymph or swinging a streamer into likely looking holds,

With its thousands of trout per river mile, the Bighorn gets the crowds but it's seldom crowded.

this is the time for you. Some say the river is to be avoided at this time because it will be high and the fishing slow. It may well be high but high water brings with it blessings of many kinds, not the least of which is that it

With its many back channels, it's not hard to find your own piece of paradise on the Bighorn.

days of their filling are filled with fish. Some days in June one can fish all day in one of these "mini Bighorns" and literally not see another boat or angler. High water also dislodges all sorts of bottom creatures from their benthic hideaways, washing them willy-nilly into the flow. The trout are not unaware of this phenomenon and take positions accordingly. The angler is well advised to be close by. And while I don't wish to proselytize for any particular time to be on the river, I would be remiss in not mentioning certain favorite times of mine. My objective in this book, you may recall, is to elucidate some of the characteristics that make the Bighorn so special.

chases away those who think that high water is synonymous with poor fishing. High water also creates seasonal channels, which within a few

SUMMER

CLOCKS AND CALENDARS HAVE little place and very little meaning on most bodies of water, and the Bighorn is no exception. Time has a way of passing until you're never quite sure where the days have gone. Suddenly, high water or low, its summertime, and indications of this fact are everywhere. The chorus of bird song, though still impressive, is largely limited to early and late in the day. The green of bankside cottonwoods have yielded their nearly incandescent glow of youth for the darker, richer, muted tones of maturity. Water temperatures are rising fast and the trout have left their cold-water retreats and have moved into the riffles and onto the flats in response

The Bighorn's low, clear water in the summer means that the successful angler is as much a hunter as a fisherman.

to their quickening metabolism. One can see them out on the flats and in the riffles, moving hungrily back and forth across the flow, greedily partaking of the cornucopia of goodies drifting by.

At this time of year, making up a large percentage of this bonanza are two particularly tasty trout morsels: the PMD or pale morning dun and the little yellow stonefly or Yellow Sally. (*Ephemerella infrequens* and *Isoperla quinquepunctatum*, respectively, for those with a scientific bent.) The annual emergence of these creatures is eagerly awaited by a host of anglers who endeavor to time their arrival on the Bighorn with that of the PMD. Some years they are successful and some years distinctly less so, for these pale little duns emerge according to some immutable riverine schedule known mostly to themselves. Most years their emergence starts somewhere between July 15 and August 1, but *E. infrequens* is at best unpredictable, and some years they don't even show up in numbers sufficient to create a fishable hatch. Many reasons have been postulated for this disparity in their number, from high water to low water and high temperatures and low temperatures to phases of the moon and other occult phenomena. I think they're just cyclical. When the hatch is on, the dry-fly fishing can range from incredible to incredibly frustrating. The first few days of this emergence the fish seem to key on duns and they are pushovers for a well-presented, high-floating dry fly. Shortly, however, whether in response

Hoppers are important on the Bighorn during some years, although the river is not known for its hopper "hatch."

to angling pressure or some unfathomable quirk in their pea-sized brain, their preference switches to various other phases of the insect's hatching cycle, none of which are imitated by a standard dry fly. It is at such times that the wizards of the fly-tying bench have their day, with such esoteric creations as cripples and floating nymphs, emergers and drowned duns. Some of these creations are marvels of fly-tying ingenuity and some even work! The old Partridge and Orange, as tied by long forgotten Englishmen, works pretty well, too.

If duns hatch, so must spinners fall, though it may happen at night if conditions for daytime egg-laying are not just right. In this case, of course, the angler is out of luck, but should he happen to be on the water when the *infrequens* spinners come down he will surely experience a moment of angling Valhalla. Even the crusty old browns who rarely come out of hiding except after dark or on exceptionally cruddy days are up and slurping greedily like youngsters. Now is the time to be here, for this fall of rusty and pale yellow spinners has to be one of the highlights of the angling year on the Bighorn.

Some years and nearly concurrent with the emergence of PMDs, the Little Yellow Sallys show up, and if you can find fish gobbling them in the riffles the dry-fly fishing can be sensational. It's also a cinch and a great confidence builder for those whose proficiency with a fly rod leaves something to be desired. The fish are most agreeable and will eat small Stimulators and various little yellow stonefly patterns with abandon.

Not so spectacular to the angler perhaps, but even more important to the trout is the little black caddis that shows up just as the PMDs and stoneflies begin to wane. *Amniocentrus* is its name, and, according to Jim Brammer who identified it as part of a masters thesis on nitrogen bubble disease, it is another of the few insects that make up 87 percent of the invertebrate biomass in the river. What this means to the trout is that caddisflies are a most reliable source of a satisfying meal and they act accordingly, feeding frantically in the riffles that these caddisflies call home. Most of this activity is subsurface, but barely so. A caddis

pupa imitation fished to a sighted feeding trout just under the surface has to be one of the most satisfying expressions of the angler's art. The same can be said for fishing sparsely hackled dry flies on slick runs a little later in the hatch.

These caddis hatches have to be experienced to be believed. Their sheer number is mind-boggling. I have experienced evenings when it is best to breath through a handkerchief to keep from inhaling your weight in caddisflies. And that's a lot of caddisflies.

All this activity takes place during full summer when the sound of bird song has been replaced by the hum of insects. The air literally vibrates with their presence. It comes across as "white noise" until you stop and

The 'Horn's trout can get quite selective in the summer, which makes fly selection critical.

Hopper time!

listen. The volume of sound is extraordinary.

Among the perpetrators of this sound is that ever-present scourge of western farmers and ranchers, the grasshopper. Grasshoppers rarely play an important role in the lives of Bighorn trout, but when they do the fishing is memorable. Nineteen eighty-six comes to mind, when a combination of factors conspired to produce the dry-fly fishing of a lifetime.

The fish got on hoppers early in July and stayed keyed on them the rest of the summer. I remember sitting on top of the Red Cliffs watching the huge, long run below. Its surface was pockmarked with little geysers whose spume blew away like spindrift in the wind as countless trout dined on countless grasshoppers. Nineteen eighty-six remains the year of the grasshopper in Bighorn lore.

While waiting for another year like 1986, don't neglect to try a hopper along fishy looking banks or in shallow riffles and tailouts of moderate speed. The results might pleasantly surprise you.

Most of us, when the fishing is so good you could cry, tend to get so involved in what we're doing that nothing matters but the fish and the fishing. This is as it should be because at this level of concentration there is no room for thoughts of boardrooms or bottom lines or for that matter, nuts and bolts. I think it's well sometimes, however, to step back from the action and pay some attention or even homage, if you will, to the singular paradise in which all this hot and heavy action is taking place. In this case of course, paradise is the Bighorn and the comparison is not without merit. Look, for example, at the streamside vegetation as you float and fish your way along. Spring's pale promise has been fulfilled and currant bushes droop with the weight of that fulfillment. Pleasing to the eye and delicious to eat, these berries of rich burgundy blue make jellies and jams of which Julia Child would be proud. Pick yourself a couple of quarts — unlike morels, there is plenty for everyone. Then get yourself a copy of Bob Krumm's excellent book, *The Rocky Mountain Berry Book,* and try some of his superb recipes. You'll be glad you did, and the

Most anglers use drift boats to get to good wading spots on the Bighorn. But the deeper water between those spots shouldn't be ignored.

resulting jellies and jams will bring back Bighorn memories. The same can also be said of streamside chokecherries and plums, which ripen somewhat later in the year. The buffalo berries that line the river

The Bighorn's riparian environment is rich in a variety of berries, such as these elderberries.

banks, though on the tart side, make great jelly. The plains Indians used them as a staple in making pemmican. Inedible except to birds, Russian olives provide a dash of silver against the otherwise lush green of stream-side vegetation, and when they're blooming in early summer the air is spicy with their fragrance. Immerse yourself in this riparian beauty and the world will seem a better place.

I've often had clients who were highly placed in the professional and corporate world tell me that no other leisure activity takes their minds off the pressures and cares of business like fly fishing. I have to agree because to do it well you must become, for a time, a predator with the intense focus and concentration that that requires. Your brain simply hasn't

room for trivialities like mergers and spreadsheets, sales meetings, impending divorces, or the futures market in pork bellies. Momentous considerations to be sure, but not to be confused with the real heavyweights like what that brown just out of casting range is eating. Patently, the overriding concerns here are how to get close without spooking him, and, having done so, what fly to offer.

Perspective is the word, and to my mind nothing lends perspective quite like a summer day spent floating a river cloaked in beauty and home to a healthy population of trout.

Sometime in August a nearly imperceptible change in the quality of light signals that summer's end is near. This change is perceived almost subliminally and cannot be explained,

but to those who spend a lot of their time floating rivers it is apparent.

Apparent also perhaps, to a smallish mayfly that generally begins its emergence about this time, though over the years I've seen them start as early as the very end of July (once) and as late as Labor Day. These tiny creatures are, of course, *Trycorithodes*, known universally among anglers as Tricos and in the Bighorn as another one of those creatures that make up such a large percentage of the river's biomass. I think Tricos provide the highlight of the dry-fly fisherman's year on a river filled with angling highlights. The reason for this is their consistency and predictability. I can't remember a year when Tricos were absent, and once their emergence starts they're out there every morning,

day after day, sometimes for as long as a couple of months. The trout are on the duns at first light or before, and you can't get on the river too early. The spinners come down after the sun has warmed things up a bit and last until about noon most days. Perhaps the best day of dry-fly fishing I've ever had occurred one unforgettable day a few years ago with my friends Rene Harrop and Dan Calahan. I don't think a moment passed between 8:00 AM and 2:00 PM when Rene or I wasn't hooked up and most of the time we both had fish on at the same time. Dan was too busy taking pictures of all this frantic action to fish much, but when he did pick up a rod it was only a matter of a cast or two before he too was engaged with Mr. Trout. It's the stuff

September's Tricos are the capstone hatch on the Bighorn.

Blizzard hatches of Tricos are common on the Bighorn. Their emergence, generally in early September, can come earlier.

Spinner From Hell. It's a huge mayfly (size 10), stygian in color whose origins are as mysterious as the Styx itself. I've never seen a nymph or a dun and have never talked to anyone who has. Those of us who speculate about such matters presume that it hatches at night. Which night is the question. Does it, like Trico, which it resembles, emerge in darkness just prior to when we see it on the water? Or does it hatch a few days earlier (which seems more likely, given its size) miles downstream and metamorph from dun to spinner many miles from where we witness its streamside dance of death and renewal. I've tried to identify it without success. But after recent conversations with Dan Gustafson, a research scientist at Montana State

of memories and winter dreams!

On one day or perhaps two or three at most during a season's Trico activity if you're very lucky to be on the river where and when it occurs, you will be treated to the fall of the

University, am led to believe it may be a *Heptagenid* of prairie rivers which normally lives out its life far from the range of any trout. Whatever it is, and in many ways I hope it remains a mystery, for we all need mysteries, the trout take note of its presence and feed like they do on nothing else. Any Bighorn angler fishing at Trico time would do well to have a few trico spinners tied on size 10 or 12 hooks in case he is lucky enough to share his place on the river with the Spinners From Hell.

Though Tricos usually begin their emergence in full summer, they generally continue emerging into autumn as miniature heralds of that most delicious of seasons.

Conscientious catch-and-release is practiced by most Bighorn regulars and by all of its veteran guides.

AUTUMN

FROM AN ANGLER'S POINT OF VIEW, autumn in Montana is as much a state of mind as it is a particular season. It has to do with peerless days of impossible blue, spent in the quest for giant browns. These are monsters that move out of mysterious holes for a brief time only, available to enchanted anglers fishing diamond rivers etched in gold. This fascination with autumn browns is part of the legacy of writers Joe Brooks and Charlie Waterman, among others, who made annual pilgrimages to rivers such as the Yellowstone and Missouri and told an enraptured fly-fishing fraternity their experiences in eloquent and persuasive prose.

They persuaded me more than once, for I was easily persuaded by matters having to do with fish. One time in particular stands out in memory. I took the girl of my dreams and headed for the Missouri in search of Mr. Big, a trout to put on the wall. While she sat in golden repose on a streamside boulder and read a book, I methodically plied the river with a streamer the size of a sparrow. Eventually my efforts were rewarded and I managed to land a brown of magisterial proportions. He was magnificent in his spawning coat of orange flame and his likeness, inscribed in pine, hangs with others

The Bighorn's swift water is deceptive to anglers, but its trout know how to use it to their full advantage.

A flotilla of Water Otter kick
boats plies the Bighorn's waters
for fall trout.

purposely harm one of my dogs. But
the memory lingers and the magic of
that glowing day lives on. And
whether the reality of autumn angling
can ever live up to its promise is
beside the point.

It is obvious that many anglers
from across the nation and the world
share this notion, for as August moves
into September a growing cadre of
anglers descends on the Bighorn
intent on sampling its autumn riches.

Manifestations of this richness
are everywhere. In dry years when low
water exposes miniature mud flats
and numerous gravel bars, shorebirds
are everywhere as they stop for a few
moments or a few days on their way
to their wintering grounds on the
sands of Padre Island or in the jungle
lagoons of Costa Rica. Joining them

of his kind on Dan Bailey's Wall of
Fame, in mute testimony to the
bounty of autumn rivers.

That was thirty years ago, a more
innocent time, and today I would no
more kill a trout like that than

Many of the Bighorn's back channels and sloughs have spring creek-like habitat that trout seek out.

they've vanished, not to be seen until the following spring. Migrating with them are the raptors. Dark accipiters, the bird hawks, lethal as winged rapiers, weave through stream-bottom cottonwoods while overhead buteos, on their way to the Argentine, play in thermals generated by stream-carved bluffs. If one is especially lucky he may witness, as I did one fall, a plunging peregrine explode a flock of teal like so many thistles in the wind. The single victim fell to earth followed by his hooded assassin.

are thousands of swallows, representing every species found regularly in North America, who use the river as a staging ground before they head south. One day they are as numerous as the fish in the river; the next day

Despite these riches the Bighorn in autumn can be somewhat disappointing to the dry-fly angler who approaches the river expecting pellucid flows and rising fish. To understand the reason for this we must look for answers in Bighorn

Lake, behind Yellowtail Dam. I believe the lack of surface activity is connected to high flows in late spring and early summer. And it also has to do with high levels of dissolved nitrogen and phosphate, which results in a huge volume of phytoplankton in the lake. Ambient light also probably plays a significant role, and a hot, dry summer seems to exacerbate the problem.

Whatever the cause, the lake turns a bright algal green, limiting visibility to a couple of feet. As fall progresses, with shorter days and cooler nights, surface water temperatures fall until they are colder than temperatures at depth. As the surface water gets colder it also gets heavier, causing it to sink, displacing warm water upward and drawing suspended algae down with it. This water flows out of the dam and into the river, greatly increasing its turbidity. During some years it turns the river a most unappealing green, something like pea soup. It's interesting that

Floating algae, the bane of trout anglers, is caused by periodic discharges from Yellowtail Dam that flush the river.

phytoplankton in the lake is a phenomenon of the upper layers of water only, since its very density limits the ability of sunlight to penetrate, thus limiting the depth at which it can grow. It's a good thing too, otherwise we'd be dealing with pea soup all summer.

A little gem I came across while researching this book is that in high-water years influent flows behind the dam cause a subsurface current that reaches all the way to the pen stocks, dragging a certain amount of suspended sediment with it. This is doubtless why the river is never as clear in years of high water as it is in years of low flows even though the lake acts as a huge settling pond.

Another factor that can adversely affect fall fishing is the sheer volume of weed, grass, and various types of moss which build up over spring and summer. The fish use it for cover and it's virtually impossible to get a fly to them when such conditions prevail. Another problem is that as temperatures drop and daylight wanes, much of this growth dies and begins to drift, further complicating fly presentation. On particularly bad days, it seems as if one is cleaning his fly of sundry drifting detritus on every cast. Don't despair though, for it is nearly axiomatic that when such conditions exist if you can find clean gravel you can find fish and lots of them. Check the shallow flats upstream of islands, fairly fast tailouts and the riffles just below them. You'll most certainly find plenty of cooperative trout.

If you pick your spots, the Bighorn is generally wader-friendly to anglers and angling companions.

Fortunately turbid water does not occur every fall, and when the river is clean there is no lovelier time to fish the Bighorn. Tricos continue to provide a moveable feast for the trout and as their numbers dwindle, they are replaced by a couple of other even tinier mayflies, *Baetis* and *Pseudocloen,* which can be categorized as tiny blue-winged olives. Except in years of lowest and clearest flows, these little guys provide minimal dry-fly fishing, but tiny nymphs fished in the riffles can produce spectacular results.

Fall signals the onset of great hatches of *Baetis* and other small mayflies that bring the river's trout to the top.

One day, be it in September or October, you will wake up to the season's first snow and a world transformed into a winter wonderland full of delightful surprises. Streamside brush and woods are alive with migrating songbirds, forced out of the sky by the cold front that brought the snow. Swallows dance over the riffles, forced by the lack of terrestrial insects to seek their sustenance from the river's bounteous larder. As you round a bend, winter's white contrasts

sharply with pale pink tamarisk and is striking under a leaden arctic sky.

The river has not escaped this transformation and as if by some wondrous legerdemain, fish are everywhere, rising to bedraggled insects paralyzed by cold and snow. These overcast days of low temperatures and subdued light have a salubrious effect on even the largest denizens of the river and they are out cruising around, looking for yet another unfortunate victim. Should they happen upon your fly, the results will be memorable. Remember that many a lunker has been landed on days that most people believe are best left to ducks and duck hunters. Knowledgeable anglers are aware of this predilection of big trout for dingy days, and an early autumn

snowfall is cause for celebration not only for its beauty but for its effect on the trout.

As wondrous as it is, September snow is about as permanent as teenage love, and clearing skies and rising temperatures signal its demise. It's replaced by that single loveliest of times in northern temperate climes, Indian Summer, with its radiant, transparent light and air so clear that if the world were flat you could look into infinity. It's a wondrous time to be afloat on the Bighorn, made doubly so by the knowledge that it's a fragile and fleeting time at best, soon to be replaced by winter. So enjoy it now, because the prospects for enjoyment are everywhere. Ducks that have skulked the summer away, hidden in marshy retreats, are out and

Overcast fall weather is perfect for blue-winged olives and brown trout on the 'Horn, as Cathy Beck demonstrates.

Of the Bighorn's many birds of prey, the peregrine falcon is the swiftest and deadliest.

you may be privileged to see a raccoon, a fox, or even a bear as you drift along. Some years when pine cone crops are meager in the high country bears are everywhere, feasting on the river's bountiful berry crop and occasionally raiding an unsuspecting angler's cooler. When a bear climbs into a boat after a snack, it doesn't bode well for any high-priced fly rods laying about and the results are, as they say, "not a pretty sight." As the river moves you toward the end of the day, listen to an airborne screech owl announce the arrival of a hunter's moon in a sky shot with arrows of rose and gold. The hush of evening is pervasive and what little breeze is left is not enough to disturb a river suddenly turned to silver and gold.

about, trying new flight feathers and forming small flocks that will soon be joined by others as their great south-bound migration begins.

River-bottom wildlife seems energized by the cold weather and

Wind is a fact of life on the northern plains, a persistent nuisance to be treated with the best possible humor. If there's ever a time it relents it's during the days of Indian Summer. The silence is profound and even the river seems muted as it flows in hushed tranquility. I've been out when it was so still I could hear a heron walking in the shallows or a trout slurping quietly against a far bank. But one of the hallmarks of Indian Summer is its brevity and soon the north wind will announce that winter is just over the horizon. Gone are the golden leaves of yesterday and cottonwoods stand stark against a sky turned wintry. The river looks sullen in its pewter opacity, but looks can be deceiving. Closer inspection will reveal that blue-winged olives are on

One of the greatest things about fall fishing on the Bighorn is that you have it almost to yourself.

the water once again and trout are everywhere, feeding voraciously.

More than once have I've sat in my duck blind peering at an empty sky above riffles alive with rising fish and wishing that the 12 gauge in my

The Bighorn has great access and it can be walked for many miles, making a drift boat optional.

hand was a 4-weight. In truth, this is the time of the famous Bighorn Blast and Cast, for ducks are everywhere and trout, as if in preparation for the lean days of winter, are feeding with greedy abandon.

The browns glowing in their speckled golden coats are particularly voracious as they restlessly move about in preparation for their annual spawning runs. Almost overnight the river has cleared of its algal turbidity and newly exposed gravel indicates where the fish have begun to dig their spawning beds.

This is the time of year to get out your "big rod" and work the long runs above and below these beds, casting a big streamer as far as strength and technique will allow. There's something atavistically satisfying about standing waist deep in a big Montana river, with the snow line low on surrounding hills, hammering a streamer the size of a squirrel into the teeth of an old-fashioned gale. Masochistic no doubt, but apart from the eighteen- to twenty-inchers that hit with some regularity, there's always the possibility that something huge will emerge from the depths to inscribe the day forever in memory.

One day when you're out on the river and its four in the afternoon and nearly dark, you realize that autumn has come and gone and you've fished your way into winter. The last migrant duck has headed south and wintering goldeneyes whistle up and down the river like so many flying penguins in their suits of black and white. If you're fortunate, you'll see a gyrfalcon make a lazy swoop at a passing flock as if in play and do a couple of barrel rolls before disappearing into a gathering snowstorm. Time now, perhaps, to let the river rest awhile in anticipation of a spring that can't be very far away.

When you locate a productive run or riffle on the Bighorn, stick with it. The river's trout often "pod up" in such water.

TECHNIQUES

THIS CHAPTER IS NOT MEANT to be a compendium of angling methods that are effective on the Bighorn. For that I highly recommend Neale Streeks' book, *Small Fly Adventures in the West,* which, with minor modifications, could have been written specifically for the Bighorn. It is an admirable guide to all the techniques, tackle, and rigs you will ever need to know, written by a pro who knows whereof he speaks.

Rather, this chapter is meant to offer a few observations in the hope that they will enhance your enjoyment of the river and perhaps assist you in taking a few fish.

There can be no argument that by far the most

Great blue herons are year-round Bighorn residents that have inexhaustible patience when hunting trout in the shallows.

effective anglers on the river are birds. The osprey, the white pelican, and the great blue heron, and each employs a different deadly method in securing its dinner. The osprey and pelican we can only admire for their prowess as they snatch their prey from the river with practiced ease and enviable results. The pelican, in fact, because of its numbers and size, could have a seriously detrimental effect on trout populations were it not for the fact that it is migratory and is only with us for a brief period in the spring.

The great blue heron, on the other hand, is with us more or less year-round and we can not only admire its angling methods, we can also imitate them. Because, unlike the osprey and the pelican, which are highly specialized fish killers, the great blue heron depends on stealth and observation for its success. These are attributes to which we can all aspire.

Notice that the heron's attire is rather subdued as it stands, poised in frozen attention at the river's edge. When it moves, it is with infinite care, eyes ever alert for the slightest movement or suggestion of a shadow that will reveal the presence of its next meal. Large trout commonly hold in extremely thin water on the river and the heron knows this well. Anyone who has fished the Bighorn for any length of time has caught plenty of fish wearing "heron scars," fish that were stabbed by that mighty spear of a bill, but escaped because they were too large for the heron to handle.

I used to be surprised that some "experts" with whom I have fished over the years would stride into the river to some particular spot that experience told them looked good, completely oblivious to the trout they were scaring as they went. I'm no longer surprised by such activity because practically everyone does it, beginner and "expert" alike. Except in the coldest month, when they are holding in deep water, trout are found in the shallowest flows. If you want to catch these fish, indeed, if you even want to be aware of their presence, you should take a page from the heron's book and move with caution and probing eyes with the sure knowledge that your efforts, like the heron's, will be rewarded. The heron's approach yields great rewards

When you spot fish working on the Bighorn, a careful stalk is required to get into casting range.

in terms of fish caught, and, more importantly, it can lead to the sheer enjoyment derived from becoming part of the river's secret world. To my mind, there are few things more satisfying in the world of fly fishing

than sneaking up on a trout until you are so close you can count his spots or touch him with your rod tip. Getting a fly to him from this range is a cinch, or should be if you've mastered the basics. Which brings us, however obliquely, to the matter of equipment and what is best for the job at hand.

As mentioned earlier, this book is not meant to be a treatise on tackle but I have some preferences that I think are worth mentioning. Over the years I have come to the still-tentative conclusion that the best all-around rod for the Bighorn is a nine-footer for a 5-weight line, with a crisp, though not super fast, action. There are most certainly better specific-purpose rods and you may for example, prefer a fast-action 3-weight for certain dry-fly applications or a slow-action nine-and-a-half foot rod for casting lead and working nymphs. The nine-foot 5-weight, however, can do most anything required of it reasonably well, from casting tiny dry flies on 6X tippets to manipulating a fair amount of line across conflicting currents. It matters little to me whether the line is a double taper or weight forward, though the weight forward is easier to cast. Any good single-action reel that holds 100 yards or so of backing will do nicely. The line should be a floater that you can see (New Zealand Specials are not necessary) and attached to it a leader of nine or ten feet, more for some conditions. Sinking lines and various wet tips have limited application on the Bighorn.

When you do everything right the Bighorn pays off, as Barry Beck demonstrates.

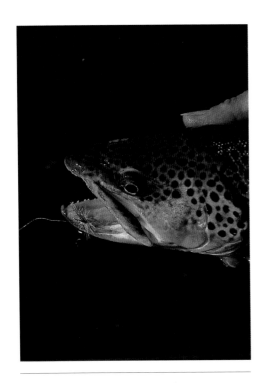

'Gator browns like this Bighorn specimen will take small dries and wets, unlike big browns in many rivers.

These will be discussed later.

Let's go back now to the trout that we have gotten so close to by moving with patience and stealth. He's there to eat and will take a properly presented fly if it's a decent approximation of the naturals on which he is feeding. You should have no trouble coming up with the correct imitation if you pay attention to the riverine world of which you are now part. For example, if there are midges around and little else, it's highly likely that our trout is feeding on midges. If he is rising, try a dry midge imitation (Midge Cluster, Griffith's Gnat, etc.) if not, a pupa drifted close should produce a strike. Bighorn midge pupae come in a vast array of colors and sizes, and you may have to experiment a bit to get the

fish to take. Incidentally, if you're in doubt about which fly to use when fishing the Bighorn and nothing seems to work despite your best efforts, try a midge pupa. It nearly always produces, if properly presented.

When fish are feeding in thin water such as we have been discussing, you're bound to spook a few, but, so what, we're not supposed to catch them all and every bungled opportunity leads to increased knowledge and improved technique. Before long you'll be successful more often than not.

Despite its well-deserved reputation as a dry-fly river, the Bighorn is, day in and day out, a wet-fly stream. Like most tailwater fisheries, the variety of insects present

On the 'Horn when all else fails, refer to hat band.

is limited but the number of each variety is astronomical. This fact simplifies things somewhat since it isn't necessary to imitate a lot of different food forms.

Scuds and sow bugs are an everyday staple, as are midge pupae and small mayfly nymphs, along with an aquatic annelid known far and wide as the San Juan Worm. If the number of aquatic forms to be imitated is limited, the number of imitations is limitless and some of them are wondrous creations indeed. The fly boxes of any Bighorn angler worth his salt bulge with artificials of rainbow hues bearing such weird and wonderful names as Chernobyl Special, Scum Bucket, Marshmallow, and how about this one — the Red-Headed Stepchild! They have in

common mainly small size and hold a particular fascination for the trout.

Weird names or not, those patterns work remarkably well and you'd be well advised to purchase or tie a selection before venturing forth on the Bighorn.

All of these patterns are normally fished on a dead drift in likely looking holds, and weight in one form or another is used to get the fly or flies to the desired depth. A strike indicator is generally employed, though in thin water all but the tiniest of them tend to scare fish. When fishing thin water instead of using a strike indicator try watching the fish. Set the hook at any movement it makes and you'll often be pleasantly surprised to find that you and the fish are attached.

The dead drift nymph fishing as commonly practiced on the Bighorn perhaps needs a bit of further explanation. It is also called the chuck-and-duck method by dry-fly purists who view it with a jaundiced eye, because it normally requires a fair bit of weight to get the fly to the bottom or to the depth at which the fish are holding. This derogatory moniker notwithstanding, it is a deadly method, or as they say, it is crude but effective. The fly is cast anywhere from straight upstream to up and across at about a 45° angle and allowed to drift naturally with the current. The line is mended more or less continuously to provide a natural drift and extend the length of that drift. If you can manage an aerial mend before the fly or flies hit the

A dead drift — nymph or dry fly — is the key to the Bighorn's trout action.

water, so much the better. This enhances your drift right from the start by placing the line upstream from the flies, allowing them to sink faster and drift more naturally. This is where the slightly slower-action rod

TECHNIQUES

Like all Bighorn trout, the rainbows are beautifully colored, well fed and in fighting shape.

this sequence the floating line hesitates even ever so slightly, the hook should be set. The chances are good you'll be fast to Mr. Trout. With practice you'll begin to perceive strikes the evidence for which is mostly subliminal. Such angling becomes high art and its expert practitioners are legendary for their prowess. Such a master was one of my early fishing companions, Chuck Fothergill, who regularly and magically produced fish from waters that I knew held no fish, like a magician pulling rabbits out of a hat. Chuck is no longer with us but he revolutionized angling methods for a generation of nymph fishermen and his fame endures. To my knowledge he never fished the Bighorn and its fish are better off for his omission.

with its ability to easily cast curves and loops of various widths comes in handy. Once the line has drifted past the angler the length of the float can be increased by shaking more line from the rod tip. If at anytime during

In addition to the patterns already mentioned, effective wet flies and nymphs include a vast assortment of midge pupal imitations, scuds in shades of pink, orange, and red in addition to its natural colors, and various sow bug patterns. It's interesting that sow bugs are so universally effective on the Bighorn, since they account for just a tiny percentage of the river's biomass. Their effectiveness as a pattern is all out of proportion to their numbers and I must conclude, if only for whimsy's sake, that they just taste good and are therefore consumed with relish by the trout. Small mayfly nymphs work well and patterns tied to imitate specific insects are, of course, particularly effective during the time of their emergence.

There just might be as many Labrador retrievers on the Bighorn as there are anglers.

If dead drift nymph fishing is a Bighorn mainstay, it is by no means the only one. A wide variety of methods are effective from time to time. For example, during caddis hatches when fish are rising

Inclement fall weather is the ticket
for connecting with one of the
'Horn's monster browns.

likely will be pointedly ignored.

Streamers often work well,
especially early and late in the season,
and a Woolly Bugger or Bighorn
Special cast to the banks and stripped
back can be effective anytime. They
are particularly effective on dark days,
early mornings, and late in the
evening. It's occasionally effective to
fish a Woolly Bugger nearly dead drift
near the bottom, jigging it slowly,
much as you would fish a nymph. It is
here that sinking lines and wet tips
come into play, and in addition to the
methods mentioned, the old standby
of working a streamer down long
runs on a sinking line sometimes
works well. It's a traditional method I
particularly like on overcast fall days
when the browns are on the prowl.

For some reason, Bighorn trout

everywhere and no dry fly in the book
works, a small soft hackle swung in
front of risers will often bring
resounding strikes. The fish are
taking fast-moving emergers just
under the surface and dry flies most

have a predilection and fondness for the color red. The precise reasons for this remain a mystery and speculation over the years has, so far, provided no answers. Terry Ross, one of my early roommates on the Bighorn, discovered this predilection and the house several of us shared in Fort Smith was soon engulfed in a haze of red detritus from our fly-tying benches. We produced great quantities of patterns that ranged from deep burnt orange to the most flamboyant fluorescent pinks and scarlets and bore names like the Fire Ant, Shrimp Cocktail and Scarlet Pimpernel. Tied in size 10 or 12, they were deadly and we enjoyed phenomenal fishing until shortly and inevitably the word got out and the trout were overwhelmed with an avalanche of red. Soon they shunned the color like the plague and the glory days of the red fly faded like the scarlet of a Bighorn sunset. As time went on the trout's natural affinity for the color has returned and red is once again a color to be reckoned with. The usefulness of size 10 and 12 hooks however is largely a thing of the past. Today you're better off using 18s and 20s. A size 20 nymph pupa tied with blood red larva lace or even red tying thread is often deadly. So too is the San Juan Worm, which was originally tied in various shades of red. It is now tied in a variety of colors that would rival Joseph's coat. I would like to briefly interject here a plea that whether you buy or tie your San Juan Worms, please avoid those tied on English bait hooks. Particularly in larger sizes,

Even at an estimated 10 percent mortality, catch-and-release fishing gives trout better odds than a stringer or creel.

An idea borrowed from Northwest steelheaders, bow-mounted catalytic heaters keep winter anglers warm and in the game on the Bighorn.

they are deadly to the trout unfortu-0nate enough to be hooked with them. A slightly curved, long-shanked hook such as the Tiemco 200 makes a great alternative, and conscientious tiers are using them exclusively.

If Bighorn Trout are catholic in their tastes with regard to subsurface food items and will eat a plethora of small artificials, the same cannot be said for their preferences in surface food. Usually, unless a hatch brings them to the surface, they ignore it altogether and the standard dry flies fished as attractors rarely evoke more than passing interest. It must be remembered that despite its freestone origins, the Bighorn, after emerging from Bighorn Canyon, is for all practical purposes a huge spring creek. For this reason, spring creek

techniques should be employed, and there are a few points about dry-fly fishing on the Bighorn I would like to emphasize. First and foremost is the fact that it is available nearly year-round, the month of June and the coldest of winter days being notable exceptions. June, because it is a period of transition between fly hatches and possibly unstable water conditions, and some winter days because it just too darn cold to fish comfortably. Comfort when fishing is, I suppose, a purely subjective matter. One morning when I was huddled in a duck blind in late December, what should my frozen eyeballs perceive but a couple of erstwhile anglers crossing the side channel below me to go fishing. It was ten below with a cold sun hanging in space like a pale

When a winter chinook wind blows through it's prime time to launch the drift boat and hit the Bighorn.

moon suspended in an opaque fog. I collected my decoys, shivering, and reflected on the lengths to which some anglers of monumental eagerness or particularly low intelligence will go to catch a trout. Not me, and I was soon home in a warm kitchen rustling up a huge breakfast of sausage and eggs.

This illustrates another significant point about the Bighorn: Because of the lake, which acts as a huge heat reservoir, water in the river is very slow to warm in the spring and just as slow to cool in the fall. Because of this fact, insect hatches and, indeed, all biological activity in the river lag at least a month behind any other comparable stream in Montana. Despite the air temperature, the anglers that unwittingly chased me from my duck blind were probably fishing in water with a temperature in the high forties or low fifties, perfectly reasonable temperatures at which to catch fish. They did, too, to which fact their gelid shouts of glee attested.

Getting back to dry-fly fishing on the Bighorn, though, I consider it second to none with which I am familiar, though I must admit to many glaring lapses in my fly-fishing experience. I have, however, talked with many well-traveled and savvy anglers and most agree that as a dry-fly stream the Bighorn is hard to beat. Its hatches, though few in number, are enormous and of long duration. Some of its insects emerge over a period of months. Black caddis and Tricos are a case in point. There are two distinct hatches of blue-winged olives and they provide great dry-fly opportunities spring and fall. Midges are on the water more or less year-round and provide the bulk of dry-fly opportunities from late fall to early summer. In addition to caddis and Tricos, summer hatches include pale morning duns, Yellow Sallys, and, for the lucky, the rare and elusive Spinner From Hell.

A further characteristic of Bighorn trout is their tendency to "pod up" when rising, especially to *Baetis* and Tricos. These pods create a distinctive surface disturbance that resembles the riffle created by a barely submerged boulder, and the number of fish in them can be quite large. The largest fish in the pod tend to be at its apex, with lesser fish lined up

Eenie, Meenie, Mynie, Moe...

irregularly behind. The trick is to pick off the bottom-most fish and work your way up until you can cast to the biggies at the pod's head. This is easier said than done, yet when the angling gods that control such

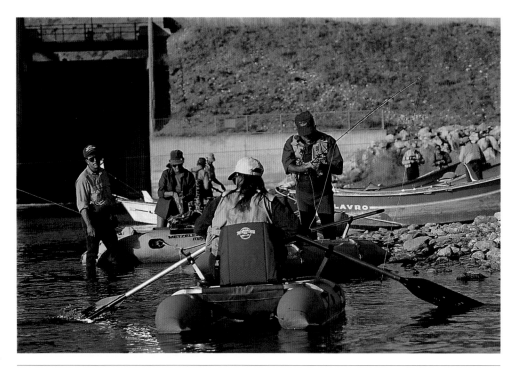

At the height of the season a little cooperation goes a long way at the Bighorn's popular afterbay boat launch.

matters are smiling it's possible to catch most of the fish in a pod before putting them down or the hatch tapers off. The memory of these days will keep you smiling for some time and your ego can bask in the rosy glow of knowing that you've done everything right.

Doing everything right on the Bighorn demands that we consider elements of behavior that have little to do with the technicalities of fishing and everything to do with its enjoyment. Because of the fact that the Bighorn is a blue-ribbon trout stream, it is crowded at times. It is a big river, however, and can handle a lot of anglers without undue strain, provided that those anglers treat each other with courtesy and respect. Our collective enjoyment of a great fishery demands nothing less. Specifically, give each angler you encounter as much room as you would like to be given consistent with conditions. The river is defined by certain riffles, runs, pools, flats, and tailouts, and it is best to leave each of these to the angler who has preceded you there.

Since streamside access is limited, boats of various descriptions are commonly used to get around on the Bighorn and there is no better way to spend a day than drifting down the river, fishing as you go. A word about their use is in order, however, and it is incumbent upon us as floaters to make sure that our boats don't infringe on the rights of others. If you can't control a boat don't use one. There is nothing that will put trout down faster than a boat drifting over their heads, and many times I've stood by in horror as a boat piloted by some well-meaning but incompetent oarsman drifted serenely over a pod of rising fish, putting them all down. Rental boats are the most egregious

Drift boats are the workhorse of the Bighorn, shuttling anglers from one great run to another.

offenders in this regard, and while they serve a useful role on the Bighorn, they should be used with discretion only by people who know how to use them. This seems a simple caveat, but I'm continually amazed at little more than scare fish. There is no way a boat can be navigated down certain channels without interfering with anglers already fishing these channels. If in doubt, park your boat and walk. The exercise will do you good and you may find a trout you would have missed had you taken your boat.

Before leaving the subject of boats and the Bighorn, I would like to plead with everyone who floats to please leave the loading ramps clear after a day on the river. Get your boat out of the water and off the ramp as quickly as possible to make room for others. If you are using a rental boat anchor it securely, well away from the ramp. It should go without saying that outfitters who rent boats have a responsibility to pick them up as

When launching on the 'Horn, drop the boat in, anchor it out of the way and clear the ramp for the next angler.

what mishandled rental boats can do to the fishing fortunes of others, to say nothing of the very real safety hazards they present. Boats of any kind should be kept out of small side channels, since when so used they do soon as possible after they are returned to the ramps, but unfortunately this quite often does not happen. It's unfortunate also that the ramps at both Three Mile and Bighorn accesses are poorly located and poorly designed. The Bighorn access ramp is downright dangerous at certain water levels, and the one at Three Mile is difficult. Perhaps the National Park Service and the Montana Department of Fish, Wildlife and Parks will do something about these ramps before someone is seriously hurt. Such action is not likely in the near future, so it is up to we users of these facilities to keep them clear so that others can use them with as much convenience and as little hazard as possible.

If boats can be a hazard on the

Golden retrievers are second in command to Labs on the Bighorn River.

Bighorn they are by any measure the best way to access and fish it. Without them much of the river would be inaccessible to anglers because it flows through the Crow reservation and non-tribal members are considered

Inflatables work well on the Bighorn, but they don't handle as well as a drift boat when the wind kicks up.

trespassers above the high-water mark. It is obvious then that a boat is necessary for fishing the Bighorn even if it is only used to access various likely looking spots that define the length of the Bighorn from the Afterbay to Mallards Landing and beyond. Indeed, good trout fishing prevails all the way to Two-Leggins Bridge. Below its confluence with Rotten Grass Creek the Bighorn is fouled by irrigation return through most of the season.

A boat can also act as a stable, maneuverable platform from which to fish the river. But, sadly, there is a group of guides who never get themselves or their clients out of their boats. It is almost as if these people are afraid of getting their feet wet. These guides seem to have their own

form of whirling disease as they row around in endless circles to fish and fish again certain deep-water hot-spots. A pass or two, it seems, ought to be sufficient to extract a couple of good fish and then on to the more interesting aspects of the game. To row back and forth through the same water until the last fish has succumbed to the net or developed a severe case of lockjaw seems to be not only excruci-atingly boring but only peripherally resembles fly fishing. Except in periods of highest flows there is little reason to fish this way. If you prefer not to fish this way, let your guide know, because some of them are probably capable of getting you into fish using legitimate fly-fishing methods.

I don't want this chapter to degenerate into a list of do's and don'ts for fishing the Bighorn, but there is one particularly heinous method of chumming up fish that I occasionally see practiced that is crude, unsportsmanlike, and harmful to the stream bed — the infamous San Juan shuffle. Again, there is no doubt that it is effective, but so are gill nets and dynamite. It is nothing less than an angler's admission that his skills are insufficient to take trout in a sporting manner.

In this chapter I've tried to present a brief overview of the river and some of the methods by which its trout can be caught. I've purposely not delved deeply into tackle and technique because to me, beyond a certain minimum skill level necessary for enjoyment, they are only ancillary to fly fishing. It is well to practice technique. Refinement and improvement of one's skills certainly provide their own rewards. The point is, though, that a beginner can have just as much fun and derive just as much pleasure from fly fishing as the most accomplished expert. A case in point is my brother Walt, an admitted tyro at the game, who last fall slipped out to the river by himself and caught a large rainbow on a tiny fly. He's still smiling, and it's my hope that in the future others like Walt will always have the Bighorn to pursue their angling dreams.

The author — an expert flyfisherman — doing field research for this book.

FUTURE

AS ONE FLOATS DOWN the Bighorn one is immediately struck by the lack of streamside development. There are no roads, and riverside homes are few and far between. In fact the banks are largely free from the encroachments of man. This salubrious state of affairs has only one reasonable explanation — the fact that the Bighorn flows through the Crow Indian Reservation. This presents some formidable obstacles to developers and one can fervently hope and pray that these obstacles remain in the future.

Toward that end, it is not too late for the Crows to consider setback laws for the length of the Bighorn within

The future of the Bighorn as a premier trout fishery depends on what we as anglers do today.

the boundaries of the reservation. The river bottom is not pristine by any means, but is relatively free from the more egregious effects of civilization and it would be best to keep it that way.

If the Crows have a vested interest in what happens along the river bank, which seems likely in view of current National Park Service efforts to transfer to tribal ownership two of the river's three prime access points, it would be in the Crow's best interest to ensure that the river continues to be the premier fly-fishing destination it is today. Construction setbacks would be a worthwhile and eminently feasible step in that direction. Interested parties such as the Bighorn River Alliance and Trout Unlimited should encourage the Crow Tribe to

consider setback laws by providing an economic benefit. Additionally, such a measure could be a positive first step in eliminating differences between those who use the Bighorn and those through whose land it flows.

At this writing, tribal ownership and administration of the Afterbay and Three Mile Access points, though not a foregone conclusion, seems likely in view of Park Service and Interior Department goals for Bighorn Canyon National Recreation Area. One of these goals is to trade the river access points to the tribe for a permanent easement across tribal lands to the National Recreation Area at OK E Beh Marina on Bighorn Lake.

Many anglers with whom I have spoken view this trade with apprehension and concern that as a consequence of such a trade, river access would be limited. In my opinion this concern is groundless since, according to Darrell Cook, superintendent of the recreation area, one of the conditions for transfer would be that public access to the river be maintained. If not, administration of the accesses would revert to the Park Service. There would doubtless be an access fee involved, but since a fee is already charged as part of a congressionally mandated Fee Demonstration Program, this is of little concern.

Of much greater concern to me is the growing number of anglers who fish the Bighorn. In view of the river's status as one of the world's great fisheries, it is hardly surprising that this is the case. The river has withstood this increasing pressure remark-ably well, but one wonders how long it can continue to do so. Perhaps it is time that the river receives some help from the Montana Game and Fish Commission in the form of restrictions on the number of anglers permitted to fish on a given day. Right now the commission lacks the authority to impose such restrictions, and has to ask the state legislature for such authority. There seems to be some interest in giving the commission this authority, but so far the legislature has refused to do so. Studies completed in 1990 by the Department of Fish, Wildlife and Parks show that the angling public overwhelmingly supports such restrictions and the department is currently working on a management plan that addresses these issues. The

Hang it over the mantle?

Bighorn River access issues are likely to be foremost and nettlesome in coming years.

just fine and there is little need for an updated plan; and the sociological issues are so complex that the department wants to consider all of the intricate ramifications of these issues before presenting the plan for public comment. Such comment, required by law, is crucial to the success of any such plan. Since any management plan is sure to draw criticism from one sector of the angling public or another, I can only applaud the department for its circumspection and caution. Nevertheless, it's time for a plan that balances the interests of the Bighorn and the diverse interests who seek enjoyment in its use. This is, of course, easier said than done, but with a bit of give and take on the part of all concerned, is within the realm of possibility.

management plan under which the Bighorn is currently managed expired in 1992 and I can only speculate that the reason a new one has not been implemented is twofold: From a biological standpoint the river is doing

Though an artificial environment in many ways, the Bighorn is obviously eminently suitable for the production of great numbers of rainbow and brown trout. But there looms the very real threat of Whirling Disease, which has so devastated several other Montana trout streams. So far there is no sign of Whirling Disease in the river, but according to Dan Gustafson, a research scientist at Montana State University, if the environmental factors are in place for the disease to thrive, then it is just a matter of time before the Bighorn is infected. Certainly the river is home to a huge population of tubifex worms, which is the prime host of the disease spores. Given the fact that most environmental factors to support

Cattle, which degrade riparian habitat, are part of the Bighorn area's economy.

Whirling Disease seem to be in place, it's only a matter of luck or perhaps isolation from infected waters that the Bighorn is not infected. It's more likely that other factors, unknown at this time, are involved. It's speculated

FUTURE

Extensive efforts are under way to keep Whirling Disease from affecting the Bighorn's trout.

that perhaps, because it is so late to warm up in the summer, the river presents a thermal barrier to the disease. This is pure speculation, and our best hope for keeping the Bighorn free from Whirling Disease is to make sure that we humans do not introduce the parasite into the river. Until we know for sure if the Bighorn is susceptible to Whirling Disease it is incumbent upon to make sure that our boats, boots, waders, and anything else that may have come in contact with contaminated water are absolutely clean before entering the Bighorn. This is especially true if one is coming from one of the Whirling Disease hotspots such as the Madison River. Again, please be careful because if we learn that the Bighorn is susceptible to Whirling Disease through its presence in the river, it will be too late.

Most outfitters and guides who rely on the Bighorn for their livelihood practice catch-and-release fishing. Whether this is a matter of principal or enlightened self-interest, it is well that they do. Otherwise, the Bighorn would soon be seriously depleted of its remarkable fish population despite its huge capacity for the production of trout. Far be it from me, however, to insist that catch-and-release fishing is a management panacea that should apply to all anglers always. It is certainly not, and keeping a few for the table is probably as good for the river as it for the angler who enjoys eating his catch. There is something particularly satisfying about eating a freshly caught trout that is all out of proportion to its worth as table fare, for the truth is that Bighorn trout are not particularly good to eat. I know

because I eat them occasionally and usually wind up telling myself never again, because to me they taste like the river in which they were raised — alkaline and redolent of the rich benthic ooze which nourishes them. Having said all this, I would simply urge that if you do keep fish to eat, exercise restraint, with an eye to the future so that your kids may enjoy the same options.

Anglers like you and I come and go, and it is my hope that our impact on the river and its creatures is as minimal as possible. Doing thus, we are doing our part to insure that the river continues to provide excellent opportunities for generations of anglers yet to come.

The Bighorn River and its fabulous trout fishing is a legacy we must preserve and pass on to future generations of anglers.

A BIGHORN BAKER'S DOZEN

I ASKED A NUMBER of the very best Bighorn River guides, whose opinions and ideas I respect, for their choice of the top dozen flies, putting my query this way: "If you were restricted to twelve patterns for the Bighorn, what would they be?"

Since the Bighorn has a limited number of aquatic invertebrates, I fully expected consensus on the subject in at least a few instances. Guides being who and what they are, however, I should have known better! In fact, no single pattern was mentioned by all. Each has his own variation on a common theme, though all agreed that the following should be imitated in some way: sowbugs, scuds, midge pupa,

caddis pupa, *Baetis* nymphs, midge clusters, and Tricos.

Most mentioned the San Juan Worm and a Woolly Bugger in several colors. Surprisingly to me, a number mentioned the grasshopper. I don't think of the Bighorn as a grasshopper river and believe they're used as widely as they apparently are because they're so much fun to fish. Since fun's the name of the game they certainly have to make the list.

Most mentioned the pale morning dun in patterns ranging from Blonde Goofus Bugs to Orange Parachutes, and Rusty Orange

Here's to the 'Horn!

Parachutes to PMD Cripples. The PMD spinner was also mentioned by several. Everyone had a dry caddis pattern of some sort on his list and a dry imitation of *Baetis* was listed by most.

Since there was such a wide variety of preference it is difficult to pare the list to only twelve patterns, so I've decided to cheat a bit and make it a baker's dozen. I do so with much trepidation, knowing full well that I'll hear about my omissions. But I do thank Kurt Collins, Mike Craig, Brad Downey, Phil Gonzalez, Ron Granamen, Hale Harris, Steve Hilbers, Bob Krumm, Richie Montella, and Gordon Rose for their assistance with my little survey and beg their forbearance.

Here is the Bighorn Top Thirteen:

1. Soft-Hackle Sow Bug
2. Scud
3. Midge Pupa
4. Black Caddis Pupa
5. Pheasant Tail
6. San Juan Worm
7. Midge Cluster
8. Blue-Winged Olive
9. Trico Spinner
10. CDC Black Caddis
11. Adult PMD pattern
12. Grasshopper
13. Woolly Bugger

BIBLIOGRAPHY

Anderson, George. "The Bighorn, Is it the Best?" *Fly Fisherman* magazine, March 1982.

Brammer, James A. "The Effects of Supersaturation of Dissolved Gases on Aquatic Invertebrates of the Bighorn River Downstream from Yellowtail Afterbay Dam." Montana State University master's thesis, 1991.

Garber, Vie Willets. "The Bozeman Trail." University of Wyoming master's thesis, 1911.

Gordon, Paul. *Bighorn Canyon National Recreation Area*, Falcon Press, Helena, MT, 1990.

Richards, Paul. *Geology of the Bighorn Canyon—Hardin Area, Montana and Wyoming*. U.S. Geological Survey Bulletin 1026, U.S. Government Printing Office, Washington D.C., 1955.

Stevenson, Harold Richard. "Trout Fishery of the Bighorn River below Yellowtail Dam, MT." Montana State University master's thesis, 1975.

Wright, John C. and Solters, Raymond A. "Limnology of Yellowtail Reservoir and the Bighorn River." Office of Research and Monitoring, U.S. Environmental Protection Agency, Washington, D.C., 1973.